Original title:
Echoes in the Ocean

Copyright © 2025 Creative Arts Management OÜ
All rights reserved.

Author: Clara Whitfield
ISBN HARDBACK: 978-1-80587-352-5
ISBN PAPERBACK: 978-1-80587-822-3

Whispers from the Wreckage

In a boat of bananas, they sailed so bright,
Coconuts laughing, what a silly sight!
Fish with sunglasses wave hello with glee,
Hopes of a treasure, just jelly in the sea.

A shark in a suit gives a cheeky grin,
Telling fishy tales of where they've been.
Octopus juggling, a comedic show,
Clams clap their shells, 'Look at him go!'

Secrets of the Seashore

Crabs wear tiny hats and strut with flair,
Sandy toes dancing, without a care.
Seashells whisper, 'Stick with the flow,'
While starfish giggle, 'We're the stars of the show!'

Turtles on surfboards, catch waves with style,
Dolphins make jokes that can last for a while.
Seaweed's a wig for the fish in the deep,
While the barnacles snore, in their slumber they keep.

The Call of the Seagulls

Seagulls squawk loudly, demanding their fries,
Their eyes darting madly, seeking big pies.
With feathers all fluffed, they boast quite a lot,
While sea turtles chuckle, 'That's a seagull plot!'

They dive for a snack, all belly and beak,
Charting a map of the best chowder sneak.
With salt in the air, they glide and they swoop,
Leaving behind a rather messy poop!

Undercurrents of Emotion

The squid writes poetry—love notes that smudge,
While fish give advice and never begrudge.
A whale sings ballads of jelly and jam,
When sea cucumbers sigh, 'Life's just a sham!'

Barnacles argue, their topic's so deep,
While the anemones laugh and just wiggle and leap.
An octopus ponders, 'What does it mean?'
When the currents of life run through seaweed green!

Murmurs Beneath the Tide

Fish in tuxedos waltz and glide,
Clams play cards, their shells open wide.
A crab jokes loud, with a pinch of glee,
While starfish cheer, 'We're not just for sea!'

The sand says, 'Shhh!' as waves crash near,
Seaweed whispers secrets, oh so clear.
A dolphin flips, with a wink and a spin,
And seagulls squawk, 'Let the fun begin!'

Reflections of a Distant Shore

The lighthouse beams like an old-time star,
It shouts, 'Hey there! I'm not that far!'
Sandcastles crumble, yet they wear a grin,
As the tide rolls in, with a mischievous spin.

The octopus juggles in the sunlight glow,
While clownfish perform a great water show.
The horizon laughs at the boats that sway,
'We're just here for the buffet!' they say.

Serenade of the Salty Breeze

A jellyfish dances, all floaty and free,
With a bowtie made from an old seaweed spree.
Seashells trumpet tunes of the vast blue spree,
While turtles roll over, giggling with glee.

The breeze tells tales of a sunken chest,
Full of trinkets from sailors who never found rest.
It tickles the fishes, causing a riot,
Chasing each other, what a wild diet!

Voices of the Deep

The whale sings softly, a lullaby tune,
While squids make faces, as silly as loons.
The coral reefs chuckle at jokes shared too loud,
In this underwater circus, oh so proud.

Anemones dance with a quirky flair,
While wrasses gossip and toss back their hair.
The deep blue giggles, a charming disguise,
Where every wave holds a surprise in its rise!

Ripples of Memory

A crab danced like it owned the shore,
With pinchers raised, it waged a war.
The seagulls laughed and took their bets,
While kids just pieced together nets.

A beach ball rolled, it took its flight,
Bouncing past, it gave a fright.
Oh look, a fish with tiny shoes,
Caught doing the cha-cha, what a view!

Lullabies from the Lighthouse

The light spins round, a disco ball,
While sailors snooze, they hear the call.
"Don't let the waves steal your last fry!"
A seagull swoops, with a sultry sigh.

As moonbeams dance on sandy floor,
They rattle dreams of tasty s'mores.
In sleepy corners, giggles sway,
As jellyfish join in for the play.

Secrets of the Currents

Fish whisper tales of coral squabbles,
While dolphins giggle and play with bubbles.
The seaweed waves, it joins the fun,
As shells compete for who's the best one.

A clam said, "I'm no ordinary snack!"
With pearls so fine, and style to back.
While crabs vote for a beachside jest,
To crown the starfish as their best.

Songs of the Saltwater

Bubbles pop to a rhythm sweet,
As barnacles tap their dancing feet.
The tides hum softly, a playful tune,
While starfish gather beneath the moon.

Octopus beats on a coral drum,
While fish cheer on, they go quite numb.
With laughter echoing through the sea,
Oh, what fun it is to just be free!

Rhythms of the Relentless Surf

The waves dance like they've had one too many,
Splashing about, getting too noisy, uncanny,
A seagull squawks, sporting a fishy grin,
Who knew the ocean's full of tails and fin?

Crabs crawl sideways, looking quite confused,
While beach balls bounce like they're just bemused,
Surfboards wobble, riders brace for a spill,
Each wave is a joke, like it's planned for a thrill.

Cadence of the Coastal Winds

The breeze comes at me with a playful shove,
It ruffles my hat like it's in a glove,
The sun's baking all, it's a sizzling day,
While wind says, 'Hold on! I'm here to play!'

A kite swoops down, entwined in my hair,
As I laugh, people scoff at the sight so rare,
The palm trees sway like they're at a dance,
Each gust throws a party, not leaving to chance.

Chants of the Coral

Beneath the waves, the fish hold a show,
Dancing in circles, putting on a glow,
The clams hum a tune, oh what a sight,
While octopuses gamble, all colors so bright.

The starfish join in with their five-pronged flair,
Waving like dancers without any care,
A lobster sidesteps, pretending to glide,
While jellyfish giggle, they just can't hide.

Reverberations from the Depths

Down in the depths, where the shadows creep,
The eels play tag, though they rarely leap,
Turtles are slow, but their jokes are the best,
With fish rolling over, they're forever blessed.

The deep sea's a circus, with barnacles cheer,
A whale sings a ballad that's silly but dear,
As bubbles escape, like they're telling a tale,
Each wave tell a story of laughter to sail.

Aria of the Aquatic Realm

The fish wear hats and dance all day,
While seaweed sways in a silly way.
Crabs play cards on a sandy shore,
Telling tales of treasures and pirate lore.

Octopus jokes make the gulls all squawk,
Even mermaids laugh at a clumsy rock.
Waves tickle toes, a splashy delight,
Under the moon, everything feels just right.

The Ocean's Timeless Ballad

A whale sings tunes, oh what a voice!
Fish form a band, they all rejoice.
Starfish tap-dance on the ocean floor,
While dolphins giggle, wanting more.

Crabs in tuxedos compete for the prize,
As jellyfish glow in their fancy ties.
The seagulls swoop with a chirpy shout,
Join the fun, they flutter about.

Distant Drums of the Sea

The shells beat drums, with a rhythmic sound,
As turtles groove, spinning round and round.
Sardines form trains, as they wiggle and spin,
It's a party where everyone can win!

Seagulls tell jokes that make the waves roll,
While otters splash water, that's their goal.
The tide pulls back, then throws a surprise,
All creatures laugh under sunny skies.

Layers of Liquid Legacy

A clam boasts loudly, a tale to tell,
While fishes giggle, all under the spell.
Coral reefs bloom with colors so bright,
As snorkeling tourists pop in for a sight.

Tidal pools shimmer with stories so grand,
Sea stars twinkle, they all lend a hand.
With laughter and joy, this realm does gleam,
A watery world, where all love to dream.

Resonance of the Rolling Waves

The sea sings songs, a splashy tune,
With crabs in tuxedos dancing by noon.
A starfish with style plays guitar on the shore,
While jellyfish juggle, begging for more.

Seagulls squawk jokes, a comedic delight,
Surfboards in rows ready for flight.
A clam with a cough joins the band on a whim,
Spinning in circles while the tide starts to skim.

Dances of the Deep Blue

Under the waves, a squid wears a hat,
While dolphins do the cha-cha with a splat.
Octopus twirls, ink flying so wide,
Blinded by moves, he's caught in the tide.

The fish throw a party, all scales and bling,
With laughter as bubbles rise up like spring.
A turtle insists he's the dance floor king,
But trips on a seaweed – oh what a fling!

Echoes of the Fathoms Below

Beneath the blue, where the sunlight fades,
Mermaids fish for gossip, swapping their grades.
A whale dreams of sushi, a light-hearted feast,
While a clownfish tells jokes, a humorous beast.

Corals are chuckling, swaying with glee,
As anemones nod, saying, "Let it be free!"
A mackerel bursts in with a punchline so bold,
And that's when the sea stars go off and get rolled.

Melodies of the Mysterious Abyss

In the depths of the sea, where shadows play tricks,
A narwhal recites rhymes with a flick.
A lobster's in pearls, feeling quite grand,
While sea cucumbers form a weird band.

The water's alive with laughter and cheer,
As crabs share anecdotes, loud and clear.
A fish in a bowtie claims he's the prime
But trips on a shell – oh what silly time!

Rhythms of the Roiling Sea

The waves crash in a silly dance,
A crab performs his clumsy prance.
Seagulls squawk, they steal my fries,
I swear they've got an evil guise.

The tide rolls in, my hat takes flight,
Swim trunks snap, oh what a sight!
Fishy friends, they wink and tease,
Even seaweed laughs with ease.

A dolphin squeaks, inviting a laugh,
While turtles chill, they take a gaff.
Mermaids giggle, their scales all bright,
Underwater antics bring pure delight.

The sunset's hues mix red and gold,
Sandy tales of treasures told.
As I sip my lemonade, I know,
This ocean's spirit steals the show.

Memories Carried by the Wind

The breeze tickles my sunburnt nose,
While kites dance high, as the wind blows.
Seashells sing with a silly tone,
Best friends are made of foam and stone.

Crabs in a race, oh what a scene,
With shells as their caps, they look so keen.
I tried to catch one, it slipped and dashed,
A comic chase, oh how we laughed!

Sandcastles built, then washed away,
With each new wave, they do not stay.
Yet laughter echoes where sand meets sea,
In the winds of time, we're wild and free.

As the sun dips low, the sky's aglow,
We share our tales, each jest we sow.
With salty lips and hearts so light,
We treasure this moment, pure delight.

The Shifting Sands of Time

With grains that tickle, they swirl and twirl,
Like mischievous pixies in a whirl.
Footprints vanish, we laugh and hop,
As the wind plays tricks, it never stops.

Infamous sand traps, once we dive,
Suddenly buried, our limbs contrive.
Beach umbrellas dance, held by the breeze,
Popping up like daisies, oh what a tease!

Time melts like ice in summer's shade,
Seashells chuckle, they've got it made.
While sunburns form, we wear them proud,
Sandy memories, we shout aloud.

As twilight falls, our giggles weave,
Into the night, where tales believe.
The stars wink down, a cosmic jest,
In the shifting sands, we find our rest.

Melodies of Melancholy Waters

Gentle ripples hum a silly tune,
While fishy friends dance just like a rune.
A lonely boat sings off-key lore,
Echoing laughter from the shore.

Sea otters juggling shells with grace,
Trying to balance, making a face.
Waves whisper secrets, they can't keep,
While the tide giggles, drifting to sleep.

The moon casts shadows, playful and light,
As jellyfish pop, a glowy sight.
Flip-flops squeak on the dampened sand,
Life's a joke we all understand.

With smiles we sail, carried by air,
Not all who wander are in despair.
In melancholy, there's a spark of cheer,
In watery realms, we forget our fear.

Whispers Beneath the Waves

A crab in a tux, so snappy,
Requests a dance, looking happy.
The fish are all laughing,
At his fancy, fun strapping.

A dolphin decides to dive low,
Wearing sunglasses just to show.
With a flip and a twist,
He says, "Don't be missed!"

The seaweed waltzes with pride,
As currents swirl, they glide.
An octopus breaks in,
Twirling with her fin.

Seagulls squawk on the scene,
As they try to be serene.
But they trip on their beaks,
While doing the freaks!

Shadows of the Deep

A starfish plays hide and seek,
With a clam, so shy and meek.
But the clam just can't see,
    The starfish's glee.

An eel wears a hat that is bright,
Flashing lights in the night.
With every shimmy and shake,
    He's the star of the lake.

Jellyfish float in a line,
Wiggling like they're in a confine.
But one got too dizzy,
    And made the rest fizzy.

A turtle tells tales so grand,
Of sea adventures unplanned.
But they laugh till they choke,
    At his one-legged joke!

Lullabies of the Tide

The waves hum a tune, so weird,
As fish gather, excited and cheered.
A shrimp sings alto, so high,
While a whale croons a sigh.

A surfer rides on a shell,
Yelling out, "I know this well!"
But he tumbles and rolls,
While seagulls steal rolls.

The tide pools hold stories untold,
A crab invents one that's bold.
He claims he once raced,
With a rival – a waste!

The barnacles clap with delight,
As the gulls call a night.
The ocean's a stage,
And laughter's the wage!

Murmurs from the Abyss

At the bottom, a fish made a bet,
On who'd find the best silhouette.
But an octopus prances,
In all of her glances!

A sardine's caught in a twist,
Claims it's part of his list.
But he flops and he flails,
As his buddy just wails.

The squid draws lines in the sand,
With a jellyfish's helping hand.
They create ocean art,
To win every heart.

An anglerfish's glow is a charm,
But his jokes cause alarm.
While the others all roll,
He's digging a hole!

Rippling Reminiscence

A fish in a hat, what a sight to see,
It winked at the waves, so cheekily.
Seagulls squawk jokes, high and spry,
While crabs dance a jig, underneath the sky.

The sandcastles stand, proud and tall,
But they melt with a laugh, as the tides call.
Shells tell tall tales, of seaweed fights,
While starfish giggle through the moonlit nights.

The Whispering Brine

A jellyfish glows like a disco ball,
It jiggles and jives, oh what a thrall!
Turtles wear shades, sipping seafoam tea,
Sardines play cards, laughing with glee.

As waves curl in whispers, secrets unwind,
They speak of a dolphin, who's terribly blind.
He trips on his tail, oh what a blunder,
While whales giggle softly, creating the thunder.

Coastal Reveries

A clam tells a joke, hidden in its shell,
Crackers all laugh, 'Oh, that's quite swell!'
Dolphins doing cartwheels, oh what a scene,
While octopuses juggle, quite the marine!

The tide pools bubble, bursting with cheer,
As the shrimp swarm around, drawing near.
Starfish take selfies, using a rock,
Posing with seagulls, tick-tock, tick-tock!

Lost Verses of the Lagoon

In a lagoon, where laughter drips,
Pelicans dance on their flimsy tips.
A lobster recites, in a high-pitched tone,
While sea cucumbers crowd with a groan.

The corals debate, who's the most bright,
While plankton twirl dull, catching some light.
With waves as their audience, echoing loud,
The tide just giggles, and takes a bow proud.

Lanterns Beneath the Blue

Beneath the waves, a light does twirl,
A fish in goggles makes a whirl.
With snickers loud, they swim in glee,
"Catch that glow! It's a jellied brie!"

The clams do chuckle, so quite odd,
While sea turtles dance and nod.
A crab in shades is quite the sight,
He pinches shrimp, a true delight!

But as they play, a storm does brew,
The starfish shout, "Who forgot the glue?"
With fins all flailing, they shout in jest,
"Next time, let's glue our hats, at best!"

And in the end, they'll share a tale,
Of lanterns bright and silly whale.
Rustling tides in a giggling spree,
Join in the fun, come swim with me!

Secrets Floating in the Breeze

A dolphin whispers a riddle bright,
To seagulls swaying in morning light.
"Why did the clam refuse to play?
It shelled itself and hides away!"

The octopus with arms so wide,
Juggles fishcakes, takes some pride.
A crabby banter makes waves crash,
At seaweed parties, they all dash!

"Why so serious?" a weakfish cries,
He wears a hat that's full of fries.
As bubbles bubble, the jelly sings,
Of seafoam cake and other flings!

Secrets swirl like cotton candy,
A mermaid laughs, her jokes are dandy.
With friendly waves and winks so sly,
The ocean giggles—oh my, oh my!

Shadows of Salt and Seaweed

Beneath the salty, dancing tide,
A sea cucumber sings with pride.
"Why do starfish never marry?
They're all too shy, oh don't you tarry!"

The seaweed sways with such a twist,
As crab and shrimp form a funny list.
"Who dropped the food?" they shout in glee,
While anemones giggle, joyful spree!

In shadows deep, the tales unfold,
Of fish with treasures—pennies, gold.
A turtle with a shell so round,
Sways like a ship—oh, what a sound!

They laugh till bubbles fill the air,
"It's hard to swim without a care!"
And as they dive, what joy they find,
In mirth and shouts, all intertwined!

A Symphony of Sailor's Whispers

A sailor grins with a fishy wink,
His sea shanties make the dolphins think.
"Why are barnacles such bad guests?
They cling too tight, they never rest!"

In the net, a cod spins a yarn,
Of tides and waves, how they can charm.
With every splash and slip and slide,
The ocean laughs, with joy and pride!

Seagulls scream and swoop for fries,
More than a lunch, it's a surprise!
With nets of laughter floating wide,
The barnacles join in, bonafide!

The whispers swirl like a sailor's cheer,
Tales of the sea that all can hear.
Sail on the waves, with heart and joy,
In laughter's bond, no sea can destroy!

Siren Songs from a Forgotten Age

In days of yore, they sang so sweet,
With fishy breath and seaweed feet.
A sailor swooned, his compass lost,
A mermaid grinned, oh what a cost!

Old barnacles, they wore with pride,
As they twirled and laughed beside,
The grumpy crab, he rolled his eyes,
While jellyfish danced beneath the skies.

A flare of gills, a swaying tail,
Their silly tunes would always fail,
To lure them in, the crew was wise,
Yet still, they'd peek with curious eyes.

So raise a toast to fins and scales,
To silly songs and ocean trails,
For in the depths, where laughter thrives,
The sweetest pranks, the fish connives.

Lost Words in the Brine

Oh salty breeze, come say a word,
The seagulls laugh, how absurd!
A clam once tried to start a speech,
But pearls rolled out, all out of reach.

Octopus with tangled pens,
Wrote silly jokes about his friends.
But ink was gone, what a disgrace,
He painted crabs all over the place!

A dolphin giggled, did a flip,
Said 'This surfboard's quite a trip!'
But when he tried to catch a wave,
He belly-flopped, and boys, oh brave!

So gather round with nets and cups,
Let laughter spill as ocean puffs,
For in the depths, we find the cheer,
Of lost words drifting far and near.

Whispers of the Waves

The tide came in with a silly grin,
As barnacles sang, 'let the fun begin!'
A wave rolled high, then crashed with flair,
Saying 'Get ready, it's time to share!'

The starfish tried to tell a joke,
But it got stuck in a swirling cloak.
With every laugh, a splash would fly,
Oh, what a sight, the tide was spry!

Seashells giggled, their echoes faint,
Telling tales of a fish named paint.
With bright colors, he'd swim and twirl,
Creating chaos in a whirl!

So dance with glee, let voices rise,
For every wave hides funny ties.
A boisterous ball where laughter reigns,
In watery depths, joy never wanes.

Soundtrack of the Sea

The ocean plays its greatest hits,
With seaweed shakin' and clammy splits.
A crab beatboxes, all crunk and loud,
While fishes form a swimming crowd.

Turtles tap-danced 'pon rock and sand,
To the surf's rhythm, all perfectly planned.
But when they slipped, oh what a show,
They gracefully flopped, like a circus flow!

A whale's low hum set the mood just right,
While dolphins darted, oh what a sight!
One tried a flip, and belly-flopped down,
As laughter echoed the whole way 'round.

So let the ocean serenade our plight,
With each silly tune, our hearts feel light.
For in its depths, where laughter rings,
The sea remains the joy that sings.

The Stillness Between the Swells

The fish do a dance with their fins so bright,
While seagulls keep squawking, a comical sight.
A jellyfish floats like a bouncy balloon,
Drifting in rhythm, a floaty festoon.

But watch out for crabs in their pinchy parade,
They'll snap at your toes—oh, the pranks they've made!
With seaweed confetti, they join in the cheer,
In a wobbly waltz that's both funny and clear.

Splashing waves giggle at the antics they see,
Where dolphins take selfies and jest like a spree.
The ocean's a circus, a wild, wavy grin,
With laughter and banter, let the fun begin!

So let's raise a shell for the jests under foam,
In the midst of the tides, we all find our home.
With frolic and folly, we dive and we play,
In the stillness that giggles, come join the ballet.

Underwater Echoes of the Past

Crabs tell old tales of the ships that went down,
While starfish roll eyes, wearing seaweed crowns.
An octopus winks with tentacles pried,
Spinning a yarn—oh, he's quite the guide!

The sunken treasures are lost, never found,
But fish gossip loudly, their tales quite profound.
With bubbles as dialogue, they chatter away,
Plotting adventures of their ocean ballet.

A flounder flops up, claiming glory of yore,
While sea cucumbers snicker from under the floor.
"Oh, the times that we had!" they say with a laugh,
Recounting their journeys, each a fun paragraph.

So listen real close, when the tide starts to swell,
You might just hear them—oh, the stories they tell!
In the watery world, there's humor so vast,
With laughter that lingers, the light from the past.

Legends of the Ocean Floor

Deep down below where the lights shimmer dim,
The squids hold a council, stirring up whim.
A narwhal plays tunes with his horn on display,
While fish join the chorus in a jolly array.

The sea urchins giggle at tales of the past,
Of sea monsters lumbering, oh how they'll last!
The coral gets cheeky, shaped like a chair,
"Sit a while, mates, and let's share a rare air."

In the shadows, the crabs play a game of charades,
Acting out legends of underwater parades.
The bubbles, they pop, in a rhythm quite neat,
As the dolphins all chime in, "Isn't this sweet?"

With puzzles and pranks in the currents they weave,
The ocean floor dances—it's hard to believe!
So join in the legends, let laughter be heard,
In this whimsical world where the absurd is preferred.

The Call of the Corals

Corals whisper secrets in colors so bright,
With fish trying to mimic, what a hilarious sight!
A clownfish is poking, "Who wore it best, guys?"
As the sea turtles chuckle, rolling their eyes.

"Hey, don't be a grouper, join in for the show!"
Says a parrotfish prancing with a vibrant glow.
Shells clack as they chime in with tunes of delight,
Swaying side to side in the ocean's moonlight.

The anemones giggle, a tickler's embrace,
While seahorses sashay, they've found their own space.
"Dance with the sea stars!" they shout with a cheer,
"In this party of currents, we banish all fear!"

So listen to the corals, their laughter runs deep,
In the swell of the waves, they promise to keep.
With humor and joy in the tide's playful call,
The ocean's own giggle will shimmer for all.

Voices Under the Surface

Bubbles rise with a giggly glee,
Fish gossip wild, just wait and see.
Underwater parties, they dance and swirl,
Telling each other tales that twirl.

Seaweed whispers secrets and jokes,
Even the clams chuckle, oh what folks!
Starfish lounge, their jokes aplenty,
With one eye closed, feeling quite minty.

Turtles roll their eyes as they go by,
"Did you hear the one about the fish who can fly?"
For every wave holds laughter galore,
Under the surface, who could ask for more?

So when you dip into the briny sea,
Remember the laughter, wild and free.
The ocean's not just deep and blue,
It's a comedy club, just for you!

Ballad of the Tide Pools

In the rocky pools, a snail sings low,
Shells echo tunes from long ago.
Crabs tap dance on the wet, slick stones,
While anemones tease with their wobbly tones.

A sea cucumber slips and lets out a laugh,
As starfish twirl, trying to do math.
"Shells don't add up to a clam's perfect date!"
Said a tiny blenny, feeling so great.

Seagulls squawking, join in the fun,
As the tide rolls in, they're never done.
Poking at shells, making them jump,
"Oh look, it's a pearl!" says the fish with a thump.

So gather 'round the tidepool show,
Where creatures collide, the laughter will flow.
In each wave's return, the joy is found,
A sing-along of the quirkiest sound!

Ghosts in the Current

The jellyfish float, looking all ghostly,
With tentacles waving quite boastfully.
"Boo!" they yell, but fish just roll eyes,
"Hard to scare us, with all those spies!"

A mackerel darts, a swift little sight,
"Can't catch my tail, so I'll swim with all might!"
The spirits giggle, a swirling tease,
As they drift along in a shimmering breeze.

"Hey, watch it!" shouts a crab with a frown,
"Stop dancing around, or we'll blow this town!"
The water's a stage for these phantoms at play,
In the current they frolic all day.

So if you wonder what lurks in the streams,
Just remember their laughter, echoing dreams.
Ghosts of the sea, with tales all aglow,
Bringing chuckles wherever they go!

Harmonies of Distant Horizons

Seashells gather for a fnny display,
As the ocean's music invites them to sway.
Crashing waves compose a zany tune,
With dolphins dancing under the moon!

The horizon chuckles at the sight it beholds,
Coral reefs shimmer in bright, bold molds.
"Is that a fish wearing a hat?" one declares,
Giggles ripple through salt-laden airs.

From the sandy shores to the salty sprays,
Under the sun, they all laugh and play.
Tides rise and fall, a comic ballet,
With sea critters bursting out in a yay!

So sail away to this humorous place,
Join in their laughter, feel the embrace.
For in every wave and each splash of sea,
The harmony sings—a giggle spree!

Driftwood Dreams

A piece of driftwood floats by me,
It whispers secrets, oh so free.
I ask it where it's been and why,
It chuckles softly, 'Not to pry.'

The jellyfish giggle as they dance,
With squishy bodies, they take a chance.
They tease the waves, then swiftly glide,
Oh, what would they do if they could ride?

Murmurs of the Moonlit Coast

The moon grins wide, a silver gleam,
While crabs play tag in a sandy dream.
A starfish cracks a joke so grand,
But seaweed just can't understand.

Shells chatter softly, a funny crew,
They argue 'bout the best ocean view.
With pretty patterns, they strut their flair,
Claiming to be the fairest, oh, beware!

Stories of the Surging Salt

The waves come crashing, a wild show,
They splash and laugh, putting on a glow.
Seagulls squawk and dive, quite bold,
Up in the air, they spin, uncontrolled.

Turtles in suits swim by with grace,
Taking their time, no need to race.
They say on land you'd trip and fall,
But in the sea, they're kings of all!

Beneath the Salted Sky

The clouds above are puffs of cream,
They float around like a daydream.
Fish below gossip in a stream,
While otters play and splash, it seems.

A whale sings out, a silly tune,
Making the dolphins dance at noon.
Under the waves, there's laughter bright,
Making the sea feel just right!

Secrets of the Nautilus

A shell with secrets tucked inside,
With whispered tales the waves confide.
It once held court with fish of lore,
Now holds my socks—I need one more!

It shimmies past a pirate groan,
Who thought the sea was his to own.
But all he found were jelly stings,
And fish that laugh while doing flings!

The captain steered with much delight,
Till a seagull stole his hat one night.
He cussed and nearly cried out loud,
As waves just bobbed—they're way too proud!

So if you spy a shell today,
Remember laughter finds its way.
For in the deep, where fish do prance,
A splash of humor leads the dance!

Reflections of Distant Shores

Where sunlight dances on the sea,
A crab wore pants—he felt so free!
He struts along the sandy beach,
In search of snacks just out of reach!

A dolphin giggles, flips and plays,
While seagulls steal his fishy trays.
They squawk and squabble for a bite,
While waves just hoot with pure delight!

A lighthouse keeper's lost his way,
He thought it was a sunny day.
But clouds above began to pout,
And suddenly, he's soaked throughout!

So when you gaze at ocean's sheen,
Remember laughter's rarely seen.
For nature jokes with waves of cheer,
A funny world, forever near!

Songs of the Sargasso

In tangled weeds where mermaids giggle,
A fish blew bubbles, made us wiggle.
They sang a tune of seaweed dreams,
Where jellyfish just danced in beams!

A crab found rhythm on the sand,
With mismatched shoes—oh, isn't that grand?
They formed a band, played clams and shells,
Which echoed through the ocean spells!

The sea turtles reorganize,
A conga line that mystifies.
They waddle forth in joyful bliss,
To dance a jig, they can't resist!

So if you hear a raucous cheer,
Know sea creatures have gathered here.
For in this world beneath the waves,
There's laughter found that always saves!

Tides of Lost Dreams

The tide rolled in with giddy glee,
As barnacles threw a jamboree.
With crabby hats and silly songs,
They twirled around the rocks like prongs!

A starfish tried to tell a tale,
But lost his grip and went off trail.
He tumbled past the coral gates,
And bumped a fish that translates!

As mermaids swim with glinting scales,
They pull a prank on passing quails.
With shells that sing and giggles loud,
They bubble up with seaweed proud!

So when you peek at waves so bright,
Listen close for sounds of light.
For in the deep, where fun abounds,
The laughter plays, and joy resounds!

Treasures of the Tranquil Deep

Bubbles rise like laughter's cheer,
Fish wear hats, oh what a sight!
A crab in shoes, he steers the pier,
Seagulls squawk, 'You dance too light!'

Seashells chat, a gossip spree,
Jellyfish float with style unmatched,
The octopus serves tea with glee,
While starfish claim by chance, they're hatched!

Turtles race in dizzy rounds,
Eels tell jokes, they twist and coil,
A sunken treasure chest abounds,
With pirate gold made out of foil!

So dive beneath and have a laugh,
Join the sea's sublime ballet,
For in this world of silly craft,
The waves will cheer for you that day!

Calling from the Kelp Forest

Underneath the wavy greens,
A sea lion twirls, what a scene!
A clam sings out in silly tunes,
While crabs play cards, oh so serene!

Kelp sways like it knows the beat,
A dolphin pranks the little fish,
With every leap, he flips, so fleet,
And all join in, the finned embellish!

Starfish do ballet but trip a lot,
Anemones giggle, sway and tease,
With all the joy that they'd forgot,
They bounce around with so much ease!

So swim among the playful throng,
Where laughter bubbles through the tide,
In this realm, you'll feel so strong,
Let the playful currents be your guide!

Murmurs of Mist and Water

Waves knock-knock upon the shore,
Seagulls squawk their cheeky lines,
Mermaids play with shells galore,
While fish crack jokes as time unwinds!

Mists drift like ghosts with silly hats,
Swaying softly in the breeze,
A crab who dances to the spats,
Makes the sun smile, with such ease!

Octopuses juggle, not a care,
While plankton giggle in nice rows,
'Did you see that? What a flair!'
'Why, yes! That's how the current flows!'

Splash into the laughter, don't be shy,
In this misty realm of pure delight,
The giggles swirl and lift you high,
As tides of humor take to flight!

The Sound of Solitude

Whispers drift where silence sings,
A lone fish hums an off-key tune,
With bubbles popping, laughter springs,
As rocks reply, they're not immune!

The lonely turtle plods along,
With thoughts of sandwiches, how grand!
He meets the jellyfish, they bond strong,
Together they form a quirky band!

Waves lap softly, strumming low,
A hidden crab plays drums on sand,
While seaweed sways to and fro,
Creating music, oh so grand!

So dive deep into that solo beat,
Where fun and silence play their role,
In this vast sea, you'll find a seat,
To laugh with solitude, a joyful soul!

Ballad of the Briny Blue

Down by the shore, a seagull sings,
While fish put on their funny flings.
Crabs dance the cha-cha, clams tap their feet,
In the briny blue, life is a treat.

A dolphin flips, wearing a grin,
Jellyfish jiggle, let the fun begin.
Octopus juggling, what a sight!
Underwater parties, day turns to night.

Starfish wear shades, in the sun's glow,
Waves play the tunes, in a rhythmic flow.
Turtles with surfboards catch all the waves,
In the briny blue, every day behaves.

So if you're in need of a laugh or two,
Dive in the ocean, join the lively crew.
Where bubbles are giggles and corals hold charms,
The sea is a jest, with its playful arms.

Notes from the Nautilus

A nautilus spins with tales to share,
In waters so deep, without a care.
Whales send postcards to fish near the bay,
Scribbled in bubbles, they dance and play.

A squid writes sonnets, ink flying bright,
Each line a splash, a joyful sight.
While sea cucumbers hold a talent show,
Wiggling their bodies, putting on a glow.

Crustaceans gossip in colorful scripts,
About the clams' tales and seaweed trips.
The currents hum tunes from the ocean's band,
A symphony written in soft, shifting sand.

So raise a shell, celebrate the fun,
Where laughter is plenty, and stress is none.
In spirals and stories, the nautilus thrives,
In notes from the deep, the ocean jives.

Soundwaves on the Seafloor

Bubbles burble with a silly sound,
As mermaids giggle while spinning around.
Starfish chorus, a quirky delight,
Grooving through algae in the pale moonlight.

Surfers of seaweed ride swells of glee,
Urchins in tutus sing high and free.
Flounders flap their fins in a dance,
While lobsters groove in a sideways prance.

Sand dollars play maracas made of gold,
Tales of treasures and legends are told.
Shells clink together in a jubilant cheer,
Joining the party of all who are near.

So dive, dive down, to join in the spree,
With laughter and joy, the only decree.
In the depths of the sea, where fun is the rule,
Soundwaves hum softly, in this aquatic school.

Portals of the Pounding Waves

In the surf's embrace, a fish takes a leap,
With snickers and splashes that wake those asleep.
Buckets and shovels wear smiles so wide,
As crabs in their cozies take joy in the tide.

Surfboards collide with a comical sound,
As dolphins and children play all around.
Seagulls act as the judges of fun,
While pirates play checkers under the sun.

The waves hug the shore with a frothy cheer,
A risqué clam dance brings everyone near.
The sand dances with sparkles of gold,
As the ocean's wild stories are playfully told.

So let's laugh together, let voices unite,
With waves full of joy, and hearts shining bright.
For in the portals where fun never wanes,
Laughter's the tide, washing away all the pains.

Serenades of the Sea Glass

The bottles sing a glassy tune,
With fishy feet, they tiptoe soon.
A crab on stage, he takes his bow,
In this strange show, we wonder how.

The waves tap dance, a splashing beat,
While starfish strut on wobbly feet.
Seagulls caw, they join the fun,
In sea glass dreams beneath the sun.

A jellyfish with polka dots,
Flips and flops in clumsy spots.
"Who needs a stage for jokes and glee?"
"Just bring some seaweed, dance with me!"

At twilight's end, the tide rolls back,
And fishy laughter fills the track.
With shimmering bits, they say goodbye,
To quirky nights 'neath starry sky.

A Symphony of Storms

The thunder claps, the seagulls squawk,
As waves perform a wobbly walk.
A whale in tux, he takes the floor,
And seafoam swirls, demanding more.

A squall spills wine, it flows like cream,
While dolphins dance, they start to dream.
"Catch my tail!" one shouts with cheer,
But ends up tumbling, far and near.

The octopus conducts the show,
With eight long arms, he steals the flow.
He waves and wiggles in his flair,
"Let's make a splash! Who wants to share?"

When storms have passed, and calm prevails,
The laughter lingers in the trails.
The bubbles pop, the sea bows low,
In a soggy opera where fish do glow.

Reef Resounds

Coral reefs hum in vibrant hues,
With clownfish donning polka-dots shoes.
A shrimp with flair, he flips and twirls,
In underwater spins, he swirls.

The parrotfish giggle, sharing tales,
Of curious crabs and slippery snails.
A turtle, slow, attempts a race,
But trips on algae; what a disgrace!

The sea cucumbers wiggle with glee,
"Why are we here?" asks one with a plea.
"Just to jive in this ocean's groove,
And bust a move, let's all approve!"

As sunlight dances through the waves,
They laugh at life, with joys that save.
A symphony made of seaweed songs,
Where every creature proudly belongs.

Tidal Tales of Transformation

With each new tide, the stories shift,
From beach to sea, a wondrous gift.
A fish that glows, tells silly jokes,
As clams giggle in their little cloaks.

The barnacles, dressed in crusty shells,
Tell of the ships and their grumpy bells.
"I once was a captain!" one clam shouts,
But is met with laughter from his pals' snouts.

A sea urchin wears a crown of spines,
Claiming the throne as the best of finds.
"I'm a royal, yes, I have great tastes,
But my kingdom's plagued by silly wastes!"

With every wave that rolls ashore,
New tales emerge; there's always more.
In this salty realm, what fun it brings,
Where laughter dances on a tide of wings.

Ballads Beneath the Blue

The fish all dance, wearing hats so bright,
They tap their fins to the moon's soft light.
A crab sings solo on a seashell stage,
While jellyfish chuckle, flipping the page.

An octopus juggles, a real sight to see,
With tentacles swirling, oh, so carefree.
The starfish giggles as it flips on its back,
The seaweed sways, joining in this act.

A dolphin wears shades, sunglasses at sea,
Making waves with jokes, so wild and free.
The shrimp throw confetti, it's quite the affair,
Making merry beneath the ocean's glare.

A clam steals the spotlight, it's a real show,
Telling tall tales of tides and of flow.
With laughter and bubbles, the crew takes a bow,
For in the deep blue, it's fun here and now!

Sonnet of the Seafoam

The waves roll in with a tickle and splash,
While sandcastles laugh, in the summer's dash.
A seagull drops fries from its beak to the sea,
The crabs dine fine, what a sight to see!

With turtlenecks on, the turtles parade,
Making fashion statements in sun and in shade.
A fish with a mustache swims with a grin,
While starfish applaud, their cheers drowned in din.

An otter plays fetch with the shells on the shore,
And whispers to clams, "Oh, give me some more!"
A whale does a belly flop, splashing quite wide,
The ocean's a theater, it's fun-filled inside.

While foam rises up with a giggle and fizz,
A sea witch dances, she's quite the whiz.
In this watery world, so silly and bright,
A comedy unfolds, under moonlit night.

Tides of Timelessness

The tide tried to tickle a passing old boat,
But it just splashed back, in a giggly float.
A lobster in bowtie asked, "What's the scoop?"
While dolphins played catch, tossing seaweed loop.

A fish with a trumpet announced a new band,
With octopus drums and clam claps so grand.
The sea cucumbers joined in the dance,
Wiggling and jiggling in oceanic trance.

The flotillas of bubbles blew tunes in the air,
While sea urchins chuckled, they didn't care.
A wave rolled by, tickling sea life amused,
In laughter we swim, a world so enthused.

With sunbeams that shimmer, all bright and alive,
Every creature here knows how to thrive.
When the tides come to play, with humor full bloom,
We wallow in joy, in this watery room!

The Voice Between the Waves

In the salty surf, there's a tale to be shared,
Of an eel in a tux who expressed he was scared.
The barnacles chirped, "Oh, you'll look divine!"
They all cracked up, the punchline was fine!

A whale made a joke, with a well-timed grunt,
And the whole ocean roared, it was quite the front.
The sand talked back, with a tickle and tease,
Making all the sea critters laugh with such ease.

A crab on a skateboard rolled by with flair,
With a wink and a smile, no worries or care.
Each splash of the tide carried giggles galore,
As the dolphins played tag, and the starfish would soar.

Amid all this joy, a mermaid chimed in,
"Life here is lovely with laughter akin!"
So let's splash about in this whimsical wave,
Where every dive down is a funny doce brave!

Chants of the Sirens

Beneath the waves, fish hold a feast,
Sipping on bubbles, the laughter increased.
With a wink and a grin, they sing on repeat,
Gorging on seaweed, it's quite a treat!

Octopus jugglers perform for a show,
While crabs do the cha-cha, oh what a glow!
A dolphin does flips, in a comical chore,
While sea turtles snore, dreaming of shore.

Seagulls join in, with their cackles so loud,
Dressed in their best, they're quite the proud crowd.
"Hey, pass that kelp!" one gull shouts with a cheer,
The sea starts to dance, oh, isn't it queer?

So come to the coast, for laughter and fun,
Where jokes ride the waves, oh, plenty to be spun!
Join the silly ballet of fish with delight,
Under the moon, they party all night!

Ripples of Forgotten Tales

In the tide's twist, a crab tells a story,
Of sandcastles lost to the waves' great glory.
He limps with a shrug; it's a humorous plight,
For shells hold the secrets, quite out of sight!

Whales make a splash, in jest, they dive deep,
While passing sea turtles, they giggle and peep.
"Did you see that?" they blubber, oh what a laugh,
As clowns of the ocean, they dance on their path!

Old bottles drift by, with fortunes unread,
One says "I'm a mermaid, with shoes made of bread!"
The fish roll their eyes, swim off with a wink,
While eels tie themselves in a knot—or a link!

The tide tells its stories, a humorous spree,
Of sea creatures planning a grand jubilee.
With bubbles and giggles, they write on the foam,
In the water's embrace, no fish feels alone!

Serenade of the Seafoam

On frothy tops, the sea sings a tune,
As crabs start a band, under the moon.
With seaweed guitars and shells as the drums,
The crowd of bright fish happily hums!

Jellyfish glisten in a glow of delight,
While squids tell tall tales throughout the night.
"Did you hear about the clam that could dance?"
The audience chuckles, all caught in a trance!

A porpoise with shades says, "Watch me do flips,"
While plankton groove to the rhythm, no slips.
"Is it getting hot, or is it just me?"
The waves join in laughter, oh what a spree!

As bubbles rise high, like laughter afloat,
The harmony plays in the sun's golden coat.
Oh, seafoam may carry the weight of the jest,
In waves of mirth, we're truly blessed!

Currents of Memory

In the depths, where the old fish meet,
They swap silly tales, both funny and sweet.
With a flick of a fin, and a chuckle so loud,
They reminisce about the grandest old crowd!

A turtle recalls, with a wiggle and grin,
The race with a crab, oh, where to begin?
"His speed was unmatched, but I took a detour,
To munch on some sea grass, who could ask for more?"

The sunfish chimes in, with a flipped-over spin,
"Remember the dolphin who fell in the fin?"
The laughter cascades, like waves on the shore,
As memories linger, they beg for encore!

With currents of humor, flowing through the blue,
Each fish brings a tale, each one's quite a view.
So dive into the depths, where giggles reside,
In the underwater laughter, let friendship abide!

Nautical Narratives

A crab told a tale of the fish that forgot,
How it swam in circles, oh what a caught!
With a wink and a wave from a nearby sea star,
"You should have seen it! He swam from afar!"

The dolphin danced with flair and delight,
Chasing its shadow by day and by night.
"I swear on this wave! I'm quite the champ!"
Yet tripped on a seaweed; oh, what a stamp!

A parrotfish raved about treasures so grand,
While a seahorse laughed, waving its fin-hand.
"I'll build you a castle, right here on the sand,"
Yet forgot his blueprints; lost in neverland!

Then an octopus grinned with eight arms spread wide,
"I catch all my snacks, you can't match my ride!"
But tangled in bubbles, it slipped and it flailed,
Now it's the catch of the day! Oh, how it wailed!

The Ocean's Ancient Hymn

The waves sang softly of fish with big dreams,
Whispers of gills and of flowing moonbeams.
But one fish proclaimed, "I'm the biggest around!"
Only to swim into a net that he found!

The gulls cawed loudly, plotting a feast,
While a clam played humble, just craving some yeast.
"I'll hide in my shell till the chaos is through!"
But every tide tickled and pulled him askew!

A turtle sat back, enjoying the show,
"Life's but a joke, just take it real slow."
While the barnacles giggled on rocks hard and dry,
Chortling as crabs scuttled by in a sigh.

Then, a fish popped up and said with a grin,
"I'll juggle the shells! Let the laughter begin!"
But disaster struck, and all shells turned to blitz,
Now he juggles in pieces; oh, what a skit!

Echoing Through the Waters

A clam held court, with pearls shining bright,
Claiming it could sing the ocean's delight.
Yet when it opened wide, only bubbles did flow,
The audience laughed; they just stole the show!

A fish tried to croon, flat note after flat,
Claiming, "I'm famous; guess where I'm at!"
But when the whales joined in, the poor fish did faint,
Now a legend of silence, an unlikely saint!

The sea cucumbers rolled with jokes they would tell,
While a shark strutted by; "No one swims quite as well!"
But a sardine piped up, "Hey, we swim as a band!"
Suddenly all swam and did a quick stand!

Then a starfish, tired of all the rough play,
Said, "I'm taking a break. No more games for today!"
But in every ripple, there echoed a cheer,
For laughter must happen whenever we're near!

Wind-Swept Melodies

The wind whistled tunes through each salty wave,
Tickling the fish, oh how they misbehave!
One sprightly goldfish swished up with a smile,
"Let's dance through the currents! Stay for a while!"

A sea turtle wobbled, trying to groove,
"When you move like me, you'll definitely prove!"
But tripped on a sea urchin, and ouch! What a scene!
Now shaking like jelly, it felt so unclean!

The jellyfish jiggled, glowing so bright,
Claiming it's the one that puts on a light!
But when the pod danced, they lit up the sea,
"Hey, look over here! Now it's a party!"

Ocean's a playground with gales full of cheer,
Swimmers and singers, all wanting to steer.
Together they twirled, with laughter to share,
In this wind-swept melody, joy filled the air!

The Tide's Forgotten Tales

A crab with dreams of being a star,
Danced on the beach, but got stuck in tar.
He called for help, with a squeaky cheer,
"Lend me a claw, let's make it clear!"

The jellyfish laughed, floating so free,
"You're a diva in the toast, my dear sea!"
With a flip and a flail, he popped right free,
Fame's elusive, even for a crab from the spree!

The waves rolled in with gossip to share,
Of a fish in a tux that had lost his hair.
"He swam too fast in a wedding bouquet,
Now he's the talk of the salty café!"

So gather round, where the tales run wild,
Where fish tell jokes and a sea turtle smiled.
In this ocean of laughter, let spirits sail,
For every tide holds a whimsical tale.

Harmonies of the Horizon

The seagulls squawk in a curious choir,
Arguing who flies the highest, the flyer.
"I saw a sandwich!" one proudly exclaimed,\n"I ate the
crust – it was truly the game!"

Bubbles danced with laughter all around,
As the fish in the reef made a bouncy sound.
"We've got a rhythm, let's surf the wave,
And start a party, oh how we rave!"

A whale with hiccups began to sing,
Notes like splashes sent ripples ping-ping.
"I've got the moves, come join my spree,
Just mind the barnacles; they'll tickle your knee!"

Under the sun's warm and silly sway,
Creatures of water keep frolicking play.
In this symphony of splashes and grins,
Each note a memory, where laughter begins.

Shimmering Songs of the Abyss

Down in the deep, where the sunlight fades,
A pufferfish burst with its unset parades.
"Look at me!" it shouted, round as a ball,
"I'm the star of the show, try not to fall!"

The octopus chuckled, flipping on cue,
"Just try to relax; you're too puffed to view!"
With arms all a-wiggling and colors ablaze,
They twirled in their dance through the underwater maze.

A kittenfish grinned with a wink and a swish,
"I've got a secret for you, oh what a wish!"
"If you bubble your troubles and keep them inside,
You'll float like a balloon – just enjoy the ride!"

So sing with the bubbles and sway with the sea,
In the depths of the blue, where all spirits flee.
For the gems of the abyss are both bright and absurd,
Each fin-tastic moment, a giggle-concurred.

Soliloquy of the Sand

Upon the shore, where the sandcastles rise,
A crab in a crown practiced royal ties.
"Bow to your ruler!" it exclaimed with glee,
"I'll decree a feast of all barbecue sea!"

The sand sighed back, warm and quite soft,
"Be careful, dear crab, don't get carried aloft!
Your crown will get blown by the winds of fate,
And then who'll eat snacks from a sand-peaked plate?"

Nearby, a clam opened its mouth to share,
"I hold pearls of wisdom, now don't you dare stare!"
It rattled on tales of its waddle to waltz,
"Fish sure do party, and boy, they have faults!"

As shells whispered secrets, the tide played along,
Creating a rhythm, a pearl of a song.
In this sandy theatre where laughter is planned,
The show goes on brightly, a whimsical land.

www.ingramcontent.com/pod-product-compliance
Lightning Source LLC
Chambersburg PA
CBHW062110280426
43661CB00086B/443